Daksha's Gourmet Spices
cookbookone
revised edition

Happy Cooking!

Daksha Narsing

www.**spicesgourmet**.com

Written by Daksha Narsing
Cover Design and layout by Amesh Narsing
Photographs by Tracey Kusiewicz

ISBN 978-0-9681253-4-2

Published by:
Daksha's Gourmet Spices
1050 11th Avenue
Williams Lake, B.C. Canada
V2G 3T9

www.spicesgourmet.com
e-mail: daksha@telus.net

Printed in Canada

To

**Bhaskar
Amesh
Pravin
&
Sarena**

Love always.

Daksha

Preface

The inspiration for creating this unique gourmet cookbook comes from the support and encouragement of my family and friends.

Creating these recipes has been a loving and fun-filled experience in my kitchen. I recall my mother saying, "having happy thoughts while cooking, helps to create delicious recipes."

This cookbook was first published in 1996 and has gone through many reprints and one revision. The desire to include professional food photographs led me to rewrite this cookbook. Many of the recipes are the same, others are improved upon.

Our company, Daksha's Gourmet Spices, sells all the spices needed to make any of the recipes in this cookbook.

For more information visit www.spicesgourmet.com.

Enjoy the flavors and aromas from my kitchen to yours.

Acknowledgements

To my husband Bhaskar who is my partner both in life and business. Thank you for your input in ensuring that these recipes are perfect. Your everlasting love and inspiration mean everything to me.

To my children Amesh, Pravin and Sarena. Thank you for your continual support, encouragement and love. Amesh, I truly appreciate the work you've done on the layout and design of this cookbook. Pravin, thank you for your work with the publishing aspect of this cookbook. Sarena, thank you for all your help with the photo shoot.

To my friend Jasminder Hothi for her contribution of the "Raas Malai" recipe.

To my best friend and editor Shelly Peel for your patience and honesty. To Anne Burrill for your suggestions and editiing. Last but not least to all my friends and students for encouraging me to create this cookbook.

Spices

Celebrated spice combinations and recipes have been handed down in our family throughout the centuries, giving my mother, grandmother and mother-in-law the knowledge they've shared with me. This cookbook is a culmination of my own recipes and those of my ancestors. I am delighted to share these wonderful recipes with you and your family and friends.

This cookbook compliments the spices that we clean and blend. We put our spices through 3 stages of sieving before they are cleaned, removing all impurities. We grind the cleaned spices and use centuries old recipes to make our blends. The seven spice blends and spices used throughout this cookbook are:

Garam Masala:

Garam means warm, masala means mixture, hence warm mixture. Many families in India have their own family recipes of garam masala. Therefore there are many variations of this mixture. Our family recipe of garam masala has been in our family for over 300 years. We use 8 spices to make our garam masala. This mixture is used mainly in meat dishes, along with Thana Jeeroo, and also in some of the lentil and daal recipes. Garam Masala is also used as a garnish in some dishes.

Thana Jeeroo:

Thana means coriander and Jeeroo means cumin, therefore it is a mixture predominently made with coriander and cumin. Thana Jeeroo is a 300 year old recipe and is used mainly in vegetarian, meat and fish dishes.

Whole Spices:

Mixture of whole spices consisting of whole green cardamoms, cloves, black peppercorns and cassia sticks (cinnamon bark). The Whole Spices are used to flavor the oil in some of the meat dishes.

Cumin Seeds:

Thin small brown seeds used for flavoring many of the vegetable dishes. Crushed cumin is also used in many of the condiments.

Black Mustard Seeds:

Small round black seeds used for flavoring potato dishes, daals and vegetable dishes. Black Mustard seeds are also used as a garnish in many vegetarian appetizers.

Red Chillie Powder:

Made with dried red chillie, ground to a fine powder. Red Chillie Powder is one of the spices which gives the food the spicy hot taste.

Turmeric Powder:

Made with dried turmeric root, ground to a fine powder. Turmeric Powder gives food a lovely yellow color and also helps with digestion. Turmeric is used in almost all of the dishes in this cookbook.

Use our natural and fresh spice blends and spices to give you the best results. Spices are available online at www.spicesgourmet.com or at select dealers listed on our website.

How to Use This Book

Throughout this cookbook many recipes call for fresh masalas. These are easy to make and can be conveniently stored in the freezer.

Instructions to prepare fresh masalas are found on the following pages:

Ginger/garlic masala   page 87
Green chillie masala   page 88
Garlic masala   page 89

Refer to the Glossary section, starting on page 104, to understand some of the Indian cooking terms and vocabulary.

Try using the Meal Suggestions section beginning on page 100, but do not be afraid to put your own combinations of meals together.

Enjoy and Happy Cooking!

Table of Contents

Table of Contents

Table of Contents

Notes

Appetizers

Appetizers

Traditional Chai (Tea)

Ingredients:

2 cups water
3 thin slices fresh ginger
2 tea bags (or ½ to 1 teaspoon loose leaf tea)
½ teaspoon chai masala
2 cups milk
sugar or honey to taste

Method:

1.   Heat water in a pot over medium heat. Add tea bags or loose leaf tea, ginger and chai masala.
2.   Bring to a boil. Add milk. Stir.
3.   Allow mixture to come to a boil. Remove from heat. Remove tea bags and serve chai immediately. Or strain chai through a tea strainer if chai is made with loose leaf tea.
4.   Add sugar or honey to taste.

Spicy Spinach Rolls (Patarya)

Ingredients:

20 – 24 large sized spinach leaves (Swiss chard)
1 cup chana flour
½ cup corn flour
3 tablespoons rice flour
3 tablespoons all purpose flour
2 tablespoons ginger/garlic masala
1 teaspoon red chillie powder
1 teaspoon turmeric powder
2 teaspoons garam masala
2 teaspoons salt
2 teaspoons sugar
juice of ½ lemon
¼ - ½ cup water
4 tablespoons oil

Method:

1. Wash and pat dry spinach leaves. Set aside.
2. In a bowl mix together chana flour, corn flour, rice flour and all purpose flour.
3. Add ginger/garlic masala, red chillie powder, garam masala, turmeric powder, salt, sugar, and lemon juice. Add water to make a thick paste.
4. Spread a thin layer of paste over the entire spinach leaf.
5. Take one side of leaf and fold to the spine. Do the same with opposite side of leaf. Spread paste on folded parts of leaf.
6. Roll spinach leaf, just like a cabbage roll. Set aside. Follow same procedure with all the remaining spinach leaves.
7. Heat oil in a frying pan on medium heat. Gently place pataryas in the pan and cook for approximately 10 to 15 minutes, turning frequently. Ensure that pataryas are evenly cooked and are crispy on the outside.

Spicy Meat Balls

Ingredients:

2 lbs ground meat (chicken, beef or lamb)
4 teaspoons ginger/garlic masala
1 teaspoon green chillie masala
2 teaspoons garam masala
2 teaspoons thana jeeroo
½ teaspoon red chillie powder
½ teaspoon turmeric powder
1 ½ teaspoons salt
2 medium onions
3 tablespoons cilantro finely chopped
7 tablespoons olive oil
1 tablespoon cider vinegar
½ cup warm water

2 cassia sticks
1 - 2 whole cardamoms
2 - 3 cloves
4 - 6 black peppercorns

Method:

1. Mix together ginger/garlic masala, green chillie masala, garam masala, thana jeeroo, red chillie powder, turmeric powder and salt with 3 tablespoons of olive oil to make a spice paste. Thoroughly blend spice paste with ground meat.
2. Allow meat to marinate for at least 2 hours in the refrigerator.
3. Grate onions. Squeeze grated onions to remove excess juice. Blend onion and 2 tablespoons chopped cilantro into meat mixture.
4. In a seperate bowl mix cider vinegar with warm water. Dampen fingers before shaping meat balls. Form meat balls into 1 to 2 inch rounds.
5. Heat 4 tablespoons olive oil in a frying pan. Add cassia sticks, cardamom, cloves and peppercorns to oil. Sauté to flavour oil.
6. Add meat balls. Cover and allow to cook for 5 minutes before stirring.
7. Allow to cook for 15 to 20 minutes or till meat balls are thoroughly cooked. Stir occasionally.
8. Garnish with 1 tablespoon chopped cilantro.

Moothya (Spicy Patties)

Ingredients:

2 cups cooked rice
1 medium grated potato
1 finely chopped onion
8 tablespoons chana flour
2 teaspoons ginger/garlic masala
½ teaspoon red chillie powder
1½ teaspoons thana jeeroo
1½ teaspoons salt
½ teaspoon turmeric powder
½ teaspoon baking powder
¼ cup water (to bind mixture)
6 - 8 tablespoons oil (for frying)

Method:

1.   In a large bowl mix together rice, grated potato*, chopped onion and chana flour.
2.   Add ginger/garlic masala, red chillie powder, thana jeeroo, turmeric powder, baking powder and salt. Mix till crumbly.
3.   Add just enough water until dough starts to bind.
4.   Make 2 ½ inch round patties, about ¼ to ½ inch thick.
5.   Place patties in a heated frying pan with 4 tablespoons of oil on medium heat.
6.   Cook patties on one side for 2 to 3 minutes. Turn patties over and cook for a further 2 to 3 minutes or till patties are golden brown. Repeat steps 4 to 6 till all the dough is used up.

*Various types of vegetables can be used, for example; leftover corn, carrots, peas etc..

Potato Snacks

Ingredients:

4 large potatoes
3 cups chana flour
3 teaspoons red chillie powder
4 teaspoons salt
juice of ½ lemon
3 cups oil (for frying)

Method

1. Boil potatoes till cooked. Mash potatoes to a smooth consistency.
2. Add chana flour, red chillie powder, salt and lemon juice to mashed potatoes to make a soft dough.
3. Heat corn oil in a deep fryer or wok, on medium heat.
4. Press dough through a ricer, in a circular hand motion over hot oil, allowing strings of dough to fall into the hot oil. Carefully turn snacks over, trying not to break the strings. Fry snacks till crispy golden brown.
5. Remove potato snacks and place in colander. Allow to cool. Store in sealed jar.

Vadas

Ingredients:

¼ cup dokra mix (see page 30)
¼ cup cream of wheat
2 tablespoons corn flour
1 tablespoon rice flour
2 teaspoons ginger/garlic masala
½ teaspoon red chillie powder
½ teaspoon turmeric powder
1 ½ teaspoons salt
½ teaspoon baking powder
1 tablespoon all purpose flour
4 - 6 tablespoons plain yogurt
1 tablespoon sour cream
2 tablespoons chopped cilantro
2 tablespoons sesame seeds
¼ cup warm water
4 cups oil (for frying)

Method:

1. In a large bowl mix together dokra mix, cream of wheat, corn flour, rice flour and all purpose flour.
2. Add ginger/garlic masala, red chillie powder, turmeric powder, baking powder and salt. Mix well.
3. Add yogurt, sour cream, cilantro, sesame seeds and water. Blend together, making a thick mixture.
4. Heat oil in a wok or deep fryer on medium heat.
5. Carefully drop small half inch balls of mixture into hot oil. Fry till vadas are crispy golden brown.

Vadas make great party snacks.

Bhajyas (Pakoras)

Ingredients:

2 ½ cups chana flour
3 teaspoons ginger/garlic masala
1 teaspoon green chillie masala
½ teaspoon turmeric powder
1 teaspoon red chillie powder
3 teaspoons garam masala
2 teaspoons salt
5 tablespoons olive oil
1 - 2 cups water
2 cups finely chopped spinach
2 medium onions chopped
4 cups oil (for frying)

Method:

1.   In a large bowl mix together chana flour, olive oil, ginger/garlic masala, green chillie masala, red chillie powder, turmeric powder, garam masala and salt.
2.   Add 1 cup water and stir. Add more water, a little at a time, while mixing until it reaches the consistency of a thick paste.
3.   Add chopped spinach and onions. Stir well.
4.   Heat oil in wok or deep fryer on medium heat. Carefully drop about a tablespoon of pakora mixture into heated oil. A small size ice-cream scoop works well.
5.   Allow Bhajyas to cook for about 2 to 3 minutes, turning occasionally. Remove Bhajyas when crispy golden brown.

Serve Bhajyas with Cilantro Chutney (page 86).

Samosas

Vegetable Filling

Ingredients:

5 - 6 medium potatoes cubed
1 medium onion chopped finely
1 teaspoon cumin seeds
4 tablespoons olive oil
2 teaspoons ginger/garlic masala
1 teaspoon green chillie masala
1 teaspoon red chillie powder
½ teaspoon turmeric powder
2 teaspoons thana jeeroo
2 teaspoons salt
1 cup frozen peas washed and drained
4 tablespoons chopped cilantro

Method:

1. Heat olive oil in a large pan. Add cumin seeds.
2. Add chopped onions. Sauté till onions are lightly browned.
3. Add cubed potatoes, ginger/garlic masala, green chillie masala, thana jeeroo, red chillie powder, turmeric powder and salt. Stir well.
4. Cover and allow to cook on low heat for 15 to 20 minutes, stirring occasionally.
5. Add peas and cook for 10 to 15 minutes or till vegetables are cooked.
6. Garnish with chopped cilantro and set aside to cool.

Continued on next page.

Samosas cont.

Ground Meat Filling

Ingredients:

3 lbs ground meat (beef, chicken, turkey or lamb)
1 large onion diced
4 teaspoons ginger/garlic masala
1 teaspoon green chillie masala
3 teaspoons garam masala
3 teaspoons thana jeeroo
2 teaspoons red chillie powder
1 teaspoon turmeric powder
2 - 3 teaspoons salt
12 tablespoons olive oil
3 tablespoons chopped cilantro

Method:

1.   Mix together ginger/garlic masala, green chillie masala, garam masala, thana jeeroo, red chillie powder, turmeric powder and salt with 4 tablespoons of olive oil to make a spice paste.
2.   Add paste to ground meat, and blend in the spices. Allow meat to marinate in the refrigerator for approximately 2 hours.
3.   Heat 4 tablespoons of olive oil in a pan. Add the marinated meat and stir until meat is browned and separated. Allow to cook on low heat till oil separates and meat is thoroughly cooked.
4.   Sauté onions in a separate pan in 4 tablespoons of olive oil.
5.   Stir in onions and chopped cilantro in the cooked ground meat. Set aside and allow to cool.

Samosas cont.

Samosa Pastry

Ingredients:

4 cups all purpose flour
1 teaspoon salt
4 tablespoons olive oil
2 to 3 cups water (to bind dough)
½ cup extra flour for rolling out
½ cup extra oil to spread on pastries

Method:

1. Mix salt, olive oil and flour till crumbly. Add just enough water to bind dough. Knead dough to the consistency of a bread dough.
2. Take 1½ inch round balls of dough and roll out with a rolling pin or a velan. Make 20 to 25 two inch flat pastry rounds.
3. Using a pastry brush, spread oil completely over the surface area of 2 inch round pastries. Sprinkle each round lightly with flour.
4. Join two, 2 inch pastry rounds together with oiled sides facing each other. Press the two together gently with your hands. These are now ready to roll again.
5. Flour both sides and roll out to about 6 – 8 inch round rotis.
6. Heat tawa or flat frying pan on medium heat. Place roti on heated tawa and cook lightly for approximately 20 seconds. Turn roti over and cook for approximately 20 seconds.
7. Remove roti and place on a clean tea towel. Separate the two rotis from each other at the point where they were joined. Pile rotis one on top of each other.

Samosas cont.

8. Cover rotis in a tea towel so that the rotis do not dry out.
9. Repeat steps 2 go 7 till all dough is all used up.
10. Cut the pile of roti into 3 inch wide strips with edges* cut at an angle. This will give the pastry a trapezoid shape (see diagram on page 24).

*Keep ends of the pastry and deep fry them until crispy golden brown. Sprinkle with salt and serve as a savory snack. Or sprinkle with cinnamon and sugar to serve as a sweet snack.

Samosas cont.

Diagram of how to cut the Roti

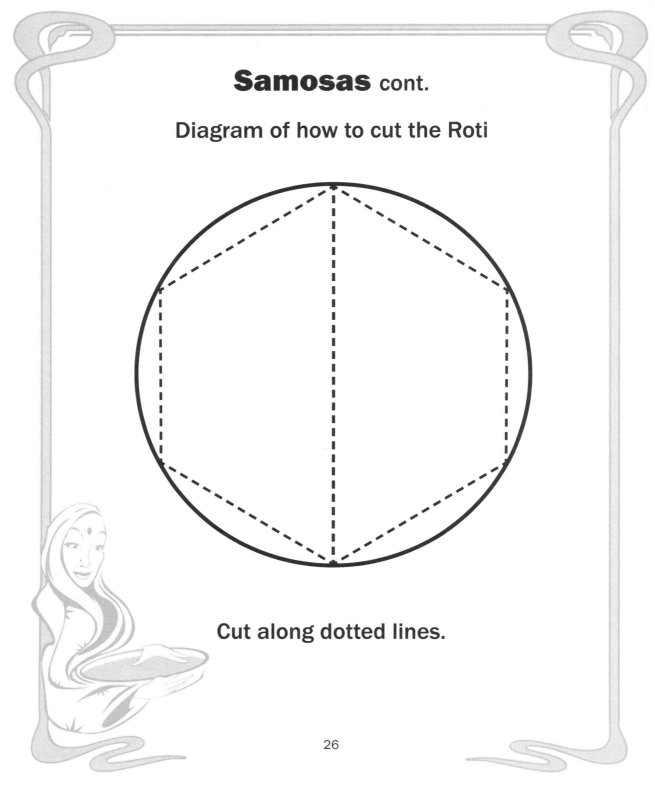

Cut along dotted lines.

Paste

Ingredients:

6 tablespoons all purpose flour
1 – 1½ cups warm water

Method for Making Paste:

1. Stir in enough water to make a paste.
2. Use a blender to mix paste thoroughly till smooth and lump free.

Method of Folding, Filling, Storing and Cooking

1. Brush paste on side A. Fold onto side B (see figure 1).
2. Apply paste on top side of side A. Fold side C onto glued area, making sure side C hangs over leaving a ½ inch flap (see figure 2).
3. Fill the samosa in the opening of the triangular pocket with approximately 1 to 1½ tablespoons filling. Brush paste on flap. Fold flap and seal Samosa (see figure 3), to make a triangular shape (see figure 4).
4. At this point Samosas can be stored and sealed in freezer bags and frozen for later use.
5. Fry Samosas in a wok or deep fryer on medium heat for 5 to 7 minutes or till Samosas are golden brown. Or bake Samosas by brushing both sides with oil or butter, (optional) on a non greased cookie sheet in a 375°F oven for 8 to 10 minutes on each side or till golden brown.

Samosas make wonderful appetizers served with cilantro chutney (page 86).

Samosas cont.

Samosa Folding Method:

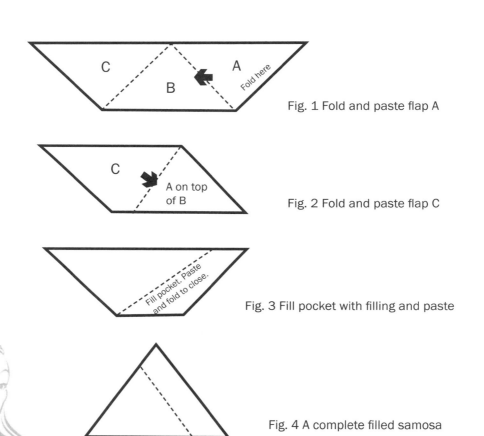

Fig. 1 Fold and paste flap A

Fig. 2 Fold and paste flap C

Fig. 3 Fill pocket with filling and paste

Fig. 4 A complete filled samosa

Pan Roasted Potatoes

Ingredients:

4 large potatoes
1 teaspoon turmeric powder
1 teaspoon salt
6 tablespoons olive oil

Method:

1. Wash and cut peeled potatoes into two inch wedges. Sprinkle turmeric powder and salt over potatoes and toss.
2. Heat olive oil in a large frying pan on medium heat and add potatoes.
3. Cook covered, stirring occasionally for about 15 to 20 minutes.
4. Remove lid and cook on low heat turning potatoes until crispy golden brown.

Dokra (Steamed Lentil Cake)

Dokra Flour Mix

Ingredients:

3 cups basmati rice
1½ cups chana daal
¾ cup urad daal

Method:

1.   In a bowl mix together basmati rice, chana daal and urad daal.
2.   Grind mixture in coffee grinder, to a grainy flour.

Continued on next page.

Dokra (Steamed Lentil Cake) cont.

Ingredients:

3¾ cups Dokra flour mix (page 30)
500 g plain yogurt
3 teaspoons finely grated ginger
½ teaspoon green chillie masala
½ teaspoon red chillie powder
½ teaspoon turmeric powder
1½ teaspoons salt
½ teaspoon baking powder
1½ cups warm water
2 tablespoons black mustard seeds
4 tablespoons shelled sesame seeds
4 tablespoons chopped cilantro
4 tablespoons unsweetened shredded coconut
4 - 6 tablespoons oil

Method:

1. Combine together in a bowl: dokra mix, yogurt, green chillie masala, ginger, red chillie powder, turmeric powder, baking powder and salt.
2. Add warm water and stir well.
3. Cover and place mixture in a cool place, for approximately 4 to 6 hours.
4. Grease 9 inch cake pans with oil.
5. Pour mixture into cake pans, filling them half full.
6. Sprinkle sesame seeds over top of mixture.
7. In a large saucepan heat enough water which covers ¼ inch depth of the saucepan. Place 2 canning jar rings, in the water. Set the pan containing dokra mixture on the rings.

Dokra (Steamed Lentil Cake) cont.

8.   Cover and allow dokra to cook for approximately 30 minutes on medium heat, making sure water does not evaporate completely. If needed add more water down the side of pan keeping water level just under the top of canning rings.

9.   To check that dokra cakes are done, poke a knife through, if it comes out clean, dokras are cooked.

10.   Remove dokra pan from pot and allow to cool. Place another cake pan with dokra mixture in the pot ensuring there is enough water at the bottom of the pan at all times. Continue steam cooking dokra until mixture is used up.

11.   Cut dokra into 2 inch squares while in the pan.

12.   In a small saucepan heat 4 tablespoons of oil. Add black mustard seeds. Allow seeds to pop.

13.   Drizzle small amounts of oil and black mustard seed mixture over the cut dokra.

14.   Garnish with chopped cilantro and shredded coconut.

15.   Remove dokra from pan and place them in a dish.

Makes approximately 4 to 6 trays of Dokras.

Serve with Traditional Chai (tea), (page 15).

Notes

Notes

Spicy Barbeques

Spicy Barbeques

Tandoori Chicken

Ingredients:

2 lbs chicken pieces (skinless)
3 teaspoons ginger/garlic masala
2 teaspoons garam masala
3 teaspoons thana jeeroo
½ teaspoon red chillie powder
1 teaspoon turmeric powder
1 teaspoon paprika
2 teaspoons salt
1½ cups of yogurt
2 tablespoons lemon juice
2 - 3 drops of red food colouring (optional)
2 tablespoons chopped cilantro
1 lime cut in wedges

Method:

1. Wash and drain chicken pieces. Mix together ginger/garlic masala, garam masala, thana jeeroo, red chillie powder, turmeric powder, paprika, salt, yogurt, lemon juice and red food colouring (optional), to make yogurt spice mixture.
2. Coat chicken with yogurt spice mixture. Cover and marinate for 3 to 6 hours in the refrigerator.
3. Barbeque chicken on medium heat. Allow chicken to cook for 5 minutes before turning.
4. Baste chicken with left over yogurt spice mixture after each turn. Cook chicken for 15 to 20 minutes or till chicken is thoroughly cooked.
5. Place Tandoori Chicken pieces on a platter and garnish with chopped cilantro and lime wedges.

Barbequed Chicken Kabobs

Ingredients:

2 lbs cubed chicken
3 teaspoons ginger/garlic masala
½ teaspoon green chillie masala
2 teaspoons garam masala
2 teaspoons thana jeeroo
1 teaspoon red chillie powder
1 teaspoon turmeric powder
1 ½ teaspoons salt
3 tablespoons olive oil
2 small zucchinis
2 cups whole mushrooms
1 cup cherry tomatoes
1 green pepper
1 package wooden skewers (pre-soaked)

Method:

1. Mix ginger/garlic masala, green chillie masala, garam masala, thana jeeroo, red chillie powder, turmeric powder, salt and olive oil to make a spice paste.
2. Marinate chicken with spice paste and place in refrigerator for 2 hours.
3. Wash and slice zucchinis into ½ inch slices. Wash and chop green peppers into 1 inch squares.
4. Soak bamboo skewers in water for ½ hour (this prevents skewers from burning). Heat barbeque on medium heat.
5. Thread sliced zucchini, green pepper, tomato and whole mushroom alternately with marinated chicken on skewers.
6. Barbecue Kabobs for 15 to 20 minutes on medium heat or till chicken is thoroughly cooked. Turn frequently.

Barbecued Fish Steaks In Lettuce Leaf

Ingredients:

5 - 6 fish steaks (salmon, cod, halibut, trout or snapper)
2 teaspoons garlic masala
½ teaspoon green chillie masala
2 teaspoons thana jeeroo
2 teaspoons ground cumin
½ teaspoon red chillie powder
½ teaspoon turmeric powder
1 teaspoon salt
3 tablespoons olive oil
1 tablespoon chopped cilantro
6 - 8 large green leaf lettuce

Method:

1. Mix garlic masala, green chillie masala, thana jeeroo, ground cumin, red chillie powder, turmeric powder and salt with olive oil to make a paste.
2. Spread paste over fish steaks. Marinate for 1 to 2 hours in the refrigerator.
3. Carefully remove lettuce leaves making sure they are intact. Use a rolling pin to flatten lettuce leaf, making the leaf pliable to work with.
4. Place marinated fish steak in the middle of the lettuce leaf. Fold leaf around fish steak and close with a toothpick. Make sure both sides of the fish steak is covered.
5. Barbecue on medium heat for 10 to 15 minutes, turning occasionally or till fish is cooked.
6. Remove and discard blackened lettuce leaves.

Barbecued Meat Balls

Ingredients:

2 lbs ground meat (chicken, beef or lamb)
4 teaspoons ginger/garlic masala
1 teaspoon green chillie masala
2 teaspoons garam masala
2 teaspoons thana jeeroo
1 teaspoon red chillie powder
1 teaspoon turmeric powder
1 ½ teaspoons salt
1 large onion
2 tablespoons olive oil
2 tablespoons chopped cilantro
3 tablespoons cider vinegar
½ cup warm water
bamboo skewers (pre-soaked)

Method:

1.   Mix ginger/garlic masala, green chillie masala, garam masala, thana jeeroo, red chillie powder, turmeric powder, salt, 2 tablespoons cider vinegar and olive oil to make a spice paste.
2.   Blend paste thoroughly with ground beef and allow to marinate for 2 hours in refrigerator.
3.   Soak bamboo skewers in water for 30 minutes.
4.   Grate onion. Gather grated onion with both hands and squeeze excess onion water out. Add squeezed onion and chopped cilantro to marinated ground meat. Blend well.
5.   Mix 1 tablespoon cider vinegar with warm water. Dampen fingers in vinegar water before shaping meat balls into 1 inch rounds.
6.   Arrange meat balls on skewers and barbecue on medium heat for 10 to 15 minutes or till meat is thoroughly cooked. Turn frequently.

Spicy Meat Balls - see page 17

Moothya (Spicy Patties) - see page 18

Bhajyas (Pakoras) - see page 21

Tandoori Chicken - see page 37

Spicy Barbecued Roasted Chicken

Ingredients:

1 whole chicken
3 teaspoons ginger/garlic masala
1 teaspoon green chillie masala
2 teaspoons garam masala
2 teaspoons thana jeeroo
1 teaspoon red chillie powder
1 teaspoon turmeric powder
2 teaspoons salt
3 tablespoons olive oil
1 whole onion peeled
1 aluminum pie plate 9"
water (for steam cooking)

Method:

1. Mix ginger/garlic masala, green chillie masala, garam masala, thana jeeroo, red chillie powder, turmeric powder and salt with olive oil to make a spice paste.
2. Rub spice paste all over the chicken including inside the cavity.
3. Place whole peeled onion inside the cavity.
4. Heat barbecue on medium heat. Place whole chicken with breast down, on the top grill of the barbecue.
5. Place pie plate under the chicken on the bottom grill. Pour enough water to fill the plate half way.
6. Close barbeque and cook for 50 to 60 minutes or till chicken is thoroughly cooked. Make sure pie plate is half filled with water, at all times, while chicken is cooking.

Spicy Barbecued Chicken Pieces

Ingredients:

3 lbs chicken pieces (skinless)
3 teaspoons ginger/garlic masala
1 teaspoon green chillie masala
2 teaspoons garam masala
2 teaspoons thana jeeroo
1 teaspoon red chillie powder
1 teaspoon turmeric powder
2 teaspoons salt
3 tablespoons olive oil
2 tablespoons chopped cilantro

Method:

1. Wash and drain chicken pieces. Mix ginger/garlic masala, green chillie masala, garam masala, thana jeeroo, red chillie powder, turmeric powder, 1 tablespoon finely chopped cilantro and salt with olive oil to make a spice paste.
2. Marinate chicken with spice paste for 2 hours in the refrigerator.
3. Heat barbecue on medium heat. Place marinated chicken pieces on grill and allow to cook for 15 to 20 minutes or till chicken is thoroughly cooked. Turn chicken frequently.
4. Remove from grill and garnish with 1 tablespoon of chopped cilantro.

Spicy Baked Potatoes

Ingredients:

4 large potatoes
1 teaspoon ginger/garlic masala
½ teaspoon red chillie powder
½ teaspoon turmeric powder
1 teaspoon ground cumin
1 teaspoon salt
1 tablespoon chopped cilantro
3 tablespoons butter

Method:

1. Scrub and wash potatoes. Core potatoes with an apple corer. Set potato cores aside in a bowl.
2. Mix together ginger/garlic masala, red chillie powder, turmeric powder, ground cumin, salt, chopped cilantro and butter, to make spiced butter.
3. Take small amounts of spiced butter and fill cored potatoes.
4. Wrap potatoes tightly in thick aluminum foil. Heat barbeque on medium heat.
5. Place all the potato cores in a foil with a teaspoon of spiced butter and warp tightly and cook with the rest of the potatoes on the barbeque.
6. Cook potatoes on the top grill of the barbeque for 25 to 30 minutes or till potatoes are thoroughly cooked. Turn potatoes frequently.

Herb Bread

Ingredients:

1 loaf french bread
3 garlic cloves grated
4 tablespoons cilantro finely chopped
½ teaspoon salt
3 teaspoons ground cumin
5 tablespoons soft butter

Method:

1. Make garlic butter by mixing together grated garlic, finely chopped cilantro, salt, ground cumin and soft butter.
2. Cut bread into ½ inch slices. Lightly spread garlic butter on both sides of bread and put loaf back together.
3. Wrap loaf in thick aluminum foil. Barbeque on medium heat for 30 to 35 minutes or bake in a preheated oven 350°F for 20 to 30 minutes.
4. Serve hot.

Spicy Meat, Poultry & Seafood Dishes

Spicy Meat, Poultry & Seafood Dishes

Chicken Pilaf

Spicy Chicken

Ingredients:

2 lbs chicken pieces (breast or thighs)
3 teaspoons ginger/garlic masala
1 teaspoon green chillie masala
2 teaspoons garam masala
2 teaspoons thana jeeroo
1 teaspoon red chillie powder
1 teaspoon turmeric powder
1 teaspoon salt
2 cassia sticks (cinnamon bark)
2 cardamoms
3 cloves
7 tablespoons olive oil

Method:

1. Mix ginger/garlic masala, green chillie masala, garam masala, thana jeeroo, red chillie powder, turmeric powder and salt with 3 tablespoons olive oil to make a paste.
2. Blend spices thoroughly with chicken and allow to marinate for 2 hours in refrigerator.
3. Heat 4 tablespoons olive oil in a deep pan. Add cassia sticks, cardamoms and cloves. Sauté to flavour the oil.
4. Add marinated chicken. Stir well. Allow to cook on medium heat for 15 to 20 minutes, stirring occasionally. Set aside.

Continued on next page.

Chicken Pilaf cont.

Basmati rice - pilaf put together

Ingredients:

2 cups basmati rice
2 teaspoons salt
5 cups water
2 tablespoons chopped cilantro

Method:

1. Wash basmati rice 3 times and cook in a pan with 4 cups of water and salt.
2. Allow rice to cook on medium heat for about 10 to 15 minutes or till rice is half cooked. Remove from the stove and drain off any excess water in a sieve. Set aside.
3. Spread half cooked rice over spicy chicken, covering completely.
4. Add 1 cup of water and cook covered on medium to low heat for 30 to 35 minutes or till both rice and chicken are thoroughly cooked.
5. Garnish with chopped cilantro.

Chicken Curry

Ingredients:

2 lbs chicken pieces
3 teaspoons ginger/garlic masala
1 teaspoon green chillie masala
2 teaspoons garam masala
2 teaspoons thana jeeroo
1 teaspoon red chillie powder
1 teaspoon turmeric powder
1½ teaspoons salt
2 medium onions chopped
1 tomato diced
1 cup tomato sauce
7 tablespoons olive oil
2 tablespoons chopped cilantro

2 cardamoms
2 cloves
4 black peppercorns
2 cassia sticks
1½ cups water

Method:

1. Mix ginger/garlic masala, green chillie masala, garam masala, thana jeeroo, red chillie powder, turmeric powder and salt with 3 tablespoons of olive oil to make a spice paste.
2. Thoroughly blend spice paste with chicken pieces and allow to marinate for 2 hours in the refrigerator.
3. Heat 4 tablespoons of olive oil in a pan and add cassia sticks, cardamoms, cloves and peppercorns to flavour the oil. Add chopped onions. Sauté.
4. Add marinated chicken and stir. Cover and cook on medium heat for 20 to 25 minutes, stirring occasionally.
5. Add diced tomatoes, tomato sauce and water. Stir.
6. Allow to cook for 20 to 30 minutes till curry is thick and chicken is thoroughly cooked. Garnish with chopped cilantro.

Bhabuti

Spicy Ground Beef

Ingredients:

1 lb ground beef
1 onion chopped
2 teaspoons ginger/garlic masala
½ teaspoon green chillie masala
2 teaspoons garam masala
2 teaspoons thana jeeroo
½ teaspoon red chillie powder
1 teaspoon turmeric powder
1 teaspoon salt
2 tablespoons chopped cilantro
7 tablespoons olive oil

Method:

1. Mix ginger/garlic masala, green chillie masala, garam masala, thana jeeroo, red chillie powder, turmeric powder, chopped cilantro and salt with 3 tablespoons olive oil to make a paste
2. Blend paste thoroughly with ground beef and allow to marinate for 2 hours in the refrigerator.
3. Heat 4 tablespoons olive oil in a pan on medium heat. Add chopped onions. Sauté.
4. Add marinated ground beef and stir well. Cover and cook for 15 to 20 minutes or till ground beef is thoroughly cooked.
5. Remove from stove and set aside.

Continued on next page.

Bhabuti cont.

Ingredients:

1 cup green onions chopped
2 cups bread crumbs
2 eggs beaten
2 cups peas (frozen)
3 carrots chopped
2 cups boiled potatoes cubed
2 cups cooked basmati rice (page 81)
½ cup water
cooked spicy ground beef (page 50)
½ cup grated cheese
1 tablespoon chopped cilantro

Method:

1. In a large bowl mix together cooked spicy ground beef, green onions, 1½ cups bread crumbs, peas, boiled potatoes, chopped carrots, cooked basmati rice and 2 eggs.
2. Transfer mixture into a 9' x 13' baking dish. Spread mixture evenly. Sprinkle water over mixture.
3. Sprinkle ½ cup of bread crumbs and grated cheese.
4. Bake in 350°F oven for 1 hour or till peas and carrots are thoroughly cooked and cheese is melted.
5. Garnish with chopped cilantro.

Spicy Roasted Chicken

Ingredients:

2 chicken pieces (thighs, legs or breasts)
3 teaspoons ginger/garlic masala
1 teaspoon green chillie masala
2 teaspoons garam masala
2 teaspoons thana jeeroo
1 teaspoon red chillie powder
1 teaspoon turmeric powder
2 teaspoons salt
3 tablespoons olive oil
1 onion peeled cut in chunks
4 medium potatoes quartered
3 carrots chopped
2 tablespoons chopped cilantro

Method:

1.   Mix ginger/garlic masala, green chillie masala, garam masala, thana jeeroo, red chillie powder, turmeric powder, 1 tablespoon chopped cilantro and 1 teaspoon salt with olive oil to make a spice paste.
2.   Thoroughly coat chicken pieces with spice paste and allow to marinate for 2 hours in the refrigerator.
3.   In a large bowl mix together chopped carrots, potatoes, onion chunks, 1 tablespoon chopped cilantro and 1 teaspoon salt. Toss.
4.   Place marinated chicken pieces in roasting a pan. Spread vegetables over chicken pieces. Cover with lid or aluminum foil.
5.   Bake in 375°F oven for 45 to 50 minutes or till chicken and vegetables are thoroughly cooked. Remove lid and broil for 5 to 10 minutes or till potatoes are golden brown.

Shrimp Curry

Ingredients:

1 lb shrimp
1 ½ teaspoons garlic masala
½ teaspoon green chillie masala
2 teaspoons ground cumin
1 ½ teaspoons thana jeeroo
½ teaspoon red chillie powder
1 teaspoon turmeric powder
1 teaspoon salt
1 cup chopped green onions
1 medium tomato diced
1 cup tomato sauce
4 tablespoons olive oil
2 tablespoons chopped cilantro

Method:

1. Heat saucepan and add tomato sauce, ½ teaspoon garlic masala, ½ teaspoon thana jeeroo, 1 teaspoon ground cumin, ¼ teaspoon red chillie powder, ½ teaspoon turmeric powder and ½ teaspoon salt. Stir.
2. Allow to cook on medium heat for 5 to 10 minutes or till sauce comes to a boil. Set aside.
3. In a seperate pan heat olive oil. Add green onions and sauté. Add diced tomatoes. Stir.
4. Add 1 teaspoon garlic masala, green chillie masala, 1 teaspoon thana jeeroo, 1 teaspoon ground cumin, ¼ teaspoon red chillie powder, ½ teaspoon turmeric powder and ½ teaspoon salt. Stir.
5. Add shrimp and stir. Allow to cook for 5 to 10 minutes on medium heat.
6. Add spiced sauce to shrimp mixture. Allow to cook for 10 to 15 minutes, or till shrimp is thoroughly cooked. Garnish with chopped cilantro.

Spicy Fish

Ingredients:

1 ½ lbs fish filleted or steak (cod, halibut, snapper, salmon or sole)
2 teaspoons garlic masala
½ teaspoon green chillie masala
2 teaspoons thana jeeroo
2 teaspoons ground cumin
½ teaspoon red chillie powder
1 teaspoon turmeric powder
1 teaspoon salt
½ teaspoon fenugreek seeds
7 tablespoons olive oil
½ cup all purpose flour
2 tablespoons chopped cilantro

Method:

1. Combine garlic masala, green chillie masala, thana jeeroo, ground cumin, red chillie powder, turmeric powder and salt with 3 tablespoons of olive oil to make a spice paste.
2. Coat fish with spice paste and marinate for 2 hours in the refrigerator.
3. Coat fish lightly with flour. Heat 4 tablespoons olive oil in a frying pan on medium heat. Add fenugreek seeds.
4. Add fish, to pan and allow to cook for 10 to 15 minutes. Turn occasionally till fish is cooked and golden brown.
5. Garnish with chopped cilantro.

Spicy Vegetable Dishes

Spicy Vegetable Dishes

Eggplant Potato Curry

Ingredients:

2 cups eggplant cut in chunks
1 potato diced
1 onion chopped finely
2 tomatoes diced
2 teaspoons ginger/garlic masala
½ teaspoon green chillie masala
1 teaspoon thana jeeroo
½ teaspoon red chillie powder
1 teaspoon turmeric powder
1 teaspoon cumin seeds
1 teaspoon salt
4 tablespoons olive oil

Method:

1. Sauté cumin seeds and chopped onion in a pot with olive oil.
2. Cut eggplant into small 1 inch chunks. Peel and dice potato to ½ inch cubes.
3. Add potato and eggplant to pot and stir.
4. Add ginger/garlic masala, green chillie masala, thana jeeroo, red chillie powder, turmeric powder and salt. Stir.
5. Cover pot with lid and allow to cook on low heat for 15 to 20 minutes stirring occasionally.
6. Add diced tomatoes and allow to cook for another 10 minutes or till all vegetables are cooked.

Potato Curry

̖d
̖ds
.rlic masala
½ tea, ̖illie masala
2 teaspoons ̖ jeeroo
½ teaspoon red chillie powder
1 teaspoon turmeric powder
1 teaspoon salt
1 medium tomato diced
½ cup tomato sauce
1 cup water
4 tablespoons olive oil
2 tablespoons cilantro chopped

Method:

1. Heat olive oil in a pan on medium heat. Add cumin seeds and chopped onions. Sauté.
2. Add diced potatoes, ginger/garlic masala, green chillie masala, thana jeeroo, red chillie powder, turmeric powder and salt. Stir well.
3. Cover and allow to cook for 10 to 15 minutes or till potatoes are cooked. Stir occasionally.
4. Add peas and allow to cook for 5 to 10 minutes. Stir.
5. Add diced tomatoes, tomato sauce and water. Allow to cook another 10 to 15 minutes. Stir.
6. Garnish with chopped cilantro.

Spicy Corn

Ingredients:

4 cups corn kernels
1 teaspoon ginger/garlic masala
½ teaspoon red chillie powder
1 teaspoon turmeric powder
1 teaspoon salt
juice of ½ lemon
1 teaspoon black mustard seeds
4 tablespoons olive oil
1 tablespoon sesame seeds
1 tablespoon chopped cilantro

Method:

1.   Heat olive oil in a pan on medium heat. Add black mustard seeds. Allow seeds to pop.
2.   Add corn, ginger/garlic masala, red chillie powder, turmeric powder, salt and lemon juice. Stir well.
3.   Allow to cook for 10 to 15 minutes on medium heat. Stir occasionally.
4.   Garnish with chopped cilantro and sesame seeds.

Spicy Pepper & Potato Dish

Ingredients:

½ green bell pepper jullienned
½ red bell pepper jullienned
2 potatoes jullienned
1 teaspoon cumin seeds
1 medium onion sliced
2 teaspoons ginger/garlic masala
1 teaspoon red chillie powder
1 teaspoon turmeric powder
1 teaspoon thana jeeroo
1 teaspoon salt
4 tablespoons olive oil
1 medium tomato
2 tablespoons chopped cilantro

Method:

1. Heat oil in a pan on medium heat. Add cumin seeds.
2. Add sliced onions. Sauté.
3. Add potatoes, ginger/garlic masala, green chillie masala, thana jeeroo, red chillie powder, turmeric powder and salt. Stir well.
4. Allow to cook for 10 minutes stirring occasionally.
5. Add green peppers and red peppers. Stir. Allow to cook for 10 to 15 minutes or till potatoes and pepper are cooked.
6. Add chopped tomatoes and allow to cook for 5 to 10 minutes. Stir occasionally.
7. Garnish with chopped cilantro.

Spicy Potatoes

Ingredients:

4 potatoes thinly sliced
1 teaspoon cumin seeds
2 teaspoons ginger/garlic masala
½ teaspoon green chillie masala
1 teaspoon thana jeeroo
½ teaspoon red chillie powder
1 teaspoon turmeric powder
1 ½ teaspoons salt
1 teaspoon black mustard seeds
6 tablespoons olive oil
2 tablespoons chopped cilantro

Method:

1. Heat olive oil in a frying pan on medium heat. Add cumin seed and black mustard seeds. Allow seeds to pop.
2. Add sliced potatoes, ginger/garlic masala, green chillie masala, thana jeeroo, red chillie powder, turmeric powder and salt. Stir well.
3. Cover and cook for 15 to 20 minutes. Stir occasionally or till potatoes are cooked and golden brown.
4. Garnish with chopped cilantro.

Notes

Spicy Lentil Dishes

Spicy Lentil Dishes

Vadhu (Sprouted Mung Bean Curry)

Ingredients:

1 cup mung beans
1 ½ onions thinly sliced
1 teaspoon ginger/garlic masala
¼ teaspoon green chillie masala
1 teaspoon thana jeeroo
½ teaspoon red chillie powder
1 teaspoon turmeric powder
1 teaspoon salt
3 ½ cups warm water
4 tablespoons olive oil

Method:

1. Soak mung beans in 3 cups of warm water in a large bowl. Soak for approximately 3 hours or till beans expand to twice their size.
2. Drain and tie beans in a clean cheesecloth or kitchen towel. Place bundle of beans in a deep dish. Store in a dark place for 10 to 12 hours or till beans have sprouted.
3. Remove sprouted beans from cloth. Wash beans gently trying not to break sprouts. Drain off excess water.
4. In a large saucepan heat oil on medium heat. Add onions and sauté.
5. Add sprouted beans, ginger/garlic masala, green chillie masala, thana jeeroo, red chillie powder, turmeric powder, ½ cup water and salt. Stir.
6. Cook in a covered pot on low heat for approximately 40 to 60 minutes. or till beans are thoroughly cooked. Stir occasionally.

Urad Toower Daal (Chevtee Daal)

Ingredients:

1 cup toower daal
1 cup urad daal
1 ½ teaspoons ginger/garlic masala
½ teaspoon green chillie masala
¼ teaspoon red chillie powder
½ teaspoon turmeric powder
1 teaspoon salt
4 tablespoons ghee (page 82)
2 teaspoons garam masala
3 - 4 cups water

Method:

1. Wash and rinse toower daal and urad daal.
2. Cook in a pressure cooker with water for 15 to 20 minutes or till daal is thoroughly cooked. Or cook daal in a large pot with water on medium heat for 40 to 60 minutes or dill daal is thoroughly cooked.
3. Strain daal through a fine sieve in a dish.
4. Add red chillie powder, turmeric powder, 1 teaspoon garam masala and salt. Stir till all spices are blended into daal.
5. In a pan melt ghee on medium heat. Add ginger/garlic masala and green chillie masala. Sauté.
6. Add daal and stir. Cover and allow daal to come to a boil. Stir constantly.
7. Sprinkle 1 teaspoon garam masala over cooked daal to garnish.

Mung Daal

Ingredients:

1 cup mung daal
1 teaspoon ginger/garlic masala
½ teaspoon green chillie masala
¼ teaspoon red chillie powder
½ teaspoon turmeric powder
½ teaspoon salt
3 tablespoons olive oil
4 to 5 cups water
1 tablespoon chopped cilantro

Method:

1.   Wash mung daal. Soak mung daal in 3 cups of water for 4 hours or till daal expands to twice its size.
2.   Wash soaked daal. Drain off water.
3.   Heat olive oil in a pan on medium heat. Add daal, ginger/garlic masala, green chillie masala, red chillie powder, turmeric powder and salt. Stir well.
4.   Add 1 to 2 cups of water, enough to cover daal.
5.   Cook on low heat for 20 to 30 minutes or till daal is cooked.
6.   Garnish with chopped cilantro.

Mung Bean Curry

Ingredients:

1 cup mung beans
1 onion finely chopped
1 tomato diced
1 ½ teaspoons ginger/garlic masala
½ teaspoon garam masala
½ teaspoon red chillie powder
1 teaspoon turmeric powder
1 teaspoon salt
3 tablespoons olive oil
3 ½ cups water

Method:

1. Wash mung beans. Cook on medium heat in a pan with 3 cups water for 30 to 40 minutes or till mung beans are thoroughly cooked. Set aside.
2. Heat olive oil in a pan and add finely chopped onions. Sauté.
3. Add tomatoes, ginger/garlic masala, red chillie powder, turmeric powder, garam masala and salt. Stir.
4. Allow to cook for 10 to 15 minutes, stirring occasionally.
5. Add cooked mung beans and ½ cup of water. Stir and cook for 15 to 20 minutes.

Zucchini With Chana Daal

Ingredients:

1 cup chana daal
1 small zucchini cut in chunks
1 teaspoon ginger/garlic masala
¼ teaspoon green chillie masala
½ teaspoon red chillie powder
1 teaspoon turmeric powder
½ teaspoon black mustard seeds
½ teaspoon salt
3 tablespoons olive oil
3 ½ cups warm water
2 tablespoons chopped cilantro

Method:

1. Soak chana daal in 3 cups warm water for about 3 hours or till daal expands to twice its original size.
2. Wash chana daal and drain off excess water. Add ginger/garlic masala, green chillie masala, red chillie powder, turmeric powder and salt. Stir well.
3. Heat olive oil in a pan on medium heat. Add black mustard seeds and allow seeds to pop in the hot oil.
4. Add chana daal and stir. Add ½ cup water. Cook covered on medium heat for 10 to 15 minutes or till daal is half cooked.
5. Add zucchini. Stir. Cover and allow to cook on low heat for another 10 to 15 minutes or till both daal and zucchini are cooked.
6. Garnish with chopped cilantro.

Spicy Black Eyed Beans

Ingredients:

1 cup black eyed beans
½ onion chopped
1 teaspoon ginger/garlic masala
1 teaspoon thana jeeroo
½ teaspoon red chillie powder
¼ teaspoon turmeric powder
1 teaspoon salt
10 to 12 ajwan seeds
4 tablespoons olive oil
1 teaspoon sweet basil
½ teaspoon oregano
½ cup tomato sauce
2 teaspoons white wine vinegar
1 tomato diced
4 ½ cups water
1 tablespoon brown sugar

Method:

1. Cook beans in 4 cups of water on medium heat for 20 to 30 minutes or till beans are fully cooked.
2. Drain beans and place in a deep dish. Add ginger/garlic masala, thana jeeroo, red chillie powder, turmeric powder and salt.
3. Heat oil in a saucepan on medium heat. Add ajwan seeds and chopped onions. Sauté.
4. Add beans and stir. Add diced tomatoes, tomato sauce, ½ cup water, vinegar, sweet basil and oregano. Stir well.
5. Add brown sugar and stir. Allow to cook for 20 to 30 minutes on low heat.

Serve with plain yogurt and naan bread or roti.

Toower Daal

Step I

Ingredients:

1 cup toower daal
1 tomato cut in chunks
¼ teaspoon red chillie powder
¼ teaspoon turmeric powder
¼ teaspoon salt
3 to 4 cups water

Method:

1. Wash daal thoroughly in warm water.
2. In a large saucepan add daal, red chillie powder, turmeric powder, salt and water.
3. Add chunks of tomato. Cook daal in a covered saucepan on medium heat for 20 to 30 minutes or till daal is cooked to a pulp. (To speed up the process cook daal in a pressure cooker for 10 to 15 minutes).
4. Strain daal through a fine sieve in a large bowl and set aside.

Continued on next page.

Toower Daal cont.

Step II

Ingredients:

Bowl of sieved toower daal (page 71)
3 teaspoons grated ginger
¾ teaspoon red chillie powder
½ teaspoon turmeric powder
juice of one lemon
1 teaspoon salt
3 whole dry red chillies
1 teaspoon black mustard seeds
1 teaspoon cumin seeds
1 ½ tablespoons brown sugar
4 tablespoons oil
1 cup water
1 tablespoon chopped cilantro

Method:

1. Add grated ginger, red chillie powder, turmeric powder, juice of one lemon and salt to sieved daal. Stir well.
2. Add water. Stir.
3. Heat oil in a separate pan on medium heat. Add whole dry red chillies, black mustard seeds and cumin seeds.
4. Add daal immediately and cover quickly to trap in flavours.
5. Cook daal till it comes to a rolling boil. Stir frequently.
6. Add brown sugar and allow to cook for 5 minutes on low heat.
7. Garnish with chopped cilantro.

Serve with basmati rice.

Indian Breads

Indian Breads

Flaky Roti (Chapatti)

Ingredients:

1 cup all purpose flour
1 cup whole wheat flour
2 tablespoons olive oil
1 teaspoon salt
1 – 2 cups hot water (to bind dough)
flour for sprinkling
oil for spreading

Method:

1. Combine all purpose flour, whole wheat flour, salt and 2 tablespoons olive oil in a bowl. Work oil into flour until crumbly. Add enough hot water to bind dough. Knead dough for 2 to 3 minutes.
2. Make 1 inch round balls. Roll out into 3 inch rounds.
3. Spread small amounts of oil completely over surface area of rounds. Sprinkle lightly with flour.
4. Fold rotis in half, spread oil on top part of rotis. Sprinkle with flour.
5. Fold rotis in half again.
6. Roll out rotis to make 6 inch flat rounds.
7. On a hot tawa cook roti lightly on one side for approximately 10 seconds. Turn roti over and cook for another 30 seconds. Turn roti over again and cook till roti puffs up, or is lightly browned.
8. Remove roti from tawa and place on a flat plate. Spread some ghee or butter on hot roti. Repeat steps 7 and 8, till finished.

Serve hot roti with many of the curry dishes in this cookbook or enjoy roti with a sprinkle of brown sugar.

Spicy Puri

Ingredients:

2 cups all purpose flour
2 teaspoons ginger/garlic masala
½ teaspoon green chillie masala
1 teaspoon red chillie powder
1 teaspoon turmeric powder
1 teaspoon salt
2 tablespoons olive oil
1 to 2 cups warm water (to bind dough)
3 to 4 cups oil for frying

Method:

1.	In a bowl combine flour, ginger/garlic masala, green chillie masala, red chillie powder, turmeric powder, salt and olive oil. Blend till mixture is crumbly. Bind dough with warm water to the consistency of a bread dough.
2.	Take handfuls of dough and roll out into large rounds about ⅛ inch thick.
3.	Using a round cookie cutter cut out round puris.
4.	Heat oil in a deep fryer or wok on medium heat.
5.	Fry several puris in hot oil. The puris will puff up into round balls. Turn puris over. Cook until crispy golden brown.
6.	Remove puris from oil and allow to cool. Store puris in a cookie jar or sealed glass container.

Serve spicy puris with Traditional chai (tea).

Sweet Puri

Ingredients:

2 cups all purpose flour
1 tablespoon sugar
1 teaspoon salt
1 tablespoon sesame seeds
8 tablespoons olive oil
1 to 2 cups warm water (to bind dough)
3 to 4 cups oil for frying

Method:

1. In a bowl combine flour, sugar, salt, sesame seeds and 3 tablespoons olive oil. Mix till flour is crumbly.
2. Bind dough with warm water to the consistency of a bread dough.
3. Take a handful of dough and roll out into one large round about ⅛ inch thick.
4. Brush olive oil and sprinkle flour lightly over surface of the dough.
5. Roll up dough like a jelly roll. Cut roll in half inch slices. Roll out each slice into 2 inch round puris.
6. Deep fry puris on medium heat in a wok or deep fryer.
7. Allow puris to puff up. Turn puris over. Cook until golden brown.
8. Remove puris from oil and place in a stainless steel colander.
9. Serve hot or cold.

Foolecha

Ingredients:

4 cups all purpose flour
2 teaspoons crushed cumin
2 teaspoons salt
2 tablespoons fast active yeast
1 tablespoon sugar
4 tablespoons olive oil
2 to 3 cups warm water (to bind dough)
3 to 4 cups oil for frying

Method:

1.   Mix together in a bowl flour, crushed cumin, fast active yeast, sugar, salt and olive oil till flour mixture is crumbly.
2.   Use only enough warm water to bind dough. Cover dough loosely with plastic food wrap. Allow dough to rise for 2 hours.
3.   Take handfuls of dough and roll out into 8 to 10 inch rounds ¼ inch thick.
4.   Cut dough with cookie cutter and set aside.
5.   Heat oil in a deep fryer or wok on medium heat.
6.   Fry in hot oil turning occasionally. Remove when foolechas are golden brown.
7.   Place foolechas in a stainless steel colander. Serve hot or cold.

Serve foolechas with many of the curry dishes in this cookbook.

Naan

Ingredients:

4 cups all purpose flour
3 teaspoons crushed cumin
2 teaspoons salt
2 tablespoons fast active yeast
1 tablespoon sugar
4 tablespoons olive oil
2 to 3 cups warm water (to bind dough)
Butter or ghee for spreading

Method:

1.   In a bowl combine flour, crushed cumin, fast active yeast, sugar, salt and olive oil. Mix till crumbly.
2.   Use enough warm water to bind dough. Cover dough loosely with plastic food wrap. Allow dough to rise for 2 hours.
3.   Make 2 inch round balls with dough. Roll into 6 inch round shapes ¼ inch thick. Cook on hot tawa or flat non-stick frying pan, on medium heat.
4.   Place naan on tawa. Cook lightly on one side for approximately 10 seconds. Turn naan over and cook till lightly browned for 20 to 30 seconds. Turn naan over again, and cook till naan puffs up.
5.   Remove from tawa and place on a flat plate. Spread butter or ghee on naan immediately.
6.   Repeat steps 3 to 5 till all of the dough is used.

Serve Naan with many of the curry dishes in this cookbook.

Plain Roti (Chapatti)

Ingredients:

1 cup all purpose flour
1 cup whole wheat flour
2 tablespoons olive oil
1 teaspoon salt
1 to 2 cups hot water (to bind dough)
ghee or butter for spreading

Method:

1. Combine all purpose flour, whole wheat flour, salt and olive oil in a bowl. Work oil into flour until crumbly. Add enough water to bind dough. Knead dough for 2 to 3 minutes.
2. Make one inch round balls. Roll out into approximately 6 inch round rotis.
3. Heat tawa (roti pan) or a non stick frying pan on medium heat. Place roti on tawa and allow to cook for 10 to 20 seconds.
4. Turn roti over and cook for 30 to 40 seconds. Turn roti over again and cook for 20 to 30 seconds or till roti puffs up.
5. Remove roti from tawa and pile rotis one on top of each other on a flat plate. Spread ghee or butter on hot roti.

Serve hot roti with any of the curry dishes in this cookbook or enjoy roti with a sprinkle of brown sugar.

Spicy Fish - see page 54

Spicy Potatoes - see page 61

Spicy Puri - see page 76

Cool Melon Dessert - see page 90

Basmati Rice

Ingredients:

1 cup basmati rice
1 teaspoon salt
3 to 4 cups water
1 tablespoon ghee or butter
¼ cup water

Method:

1. Wash* basmati rice 3 times in warm water till water is clear. Put washed rice in a large pot.
2. Cook rice on medium heat with approximately 3 to 4 cups of water.
3. Add salt and stir. Cook for 10 to 15 minutes or till rice is half cooked.
4. Drain rice in a colander. Set aside.
5. Coat bottom of the pot with ½ tablespoon ghee or butter. Add drained rice. Spread ½ tablespoon ghee or butter on top of rice.
6. Add ¼ cup of water. Cover and cook for 10 to 15 minutes on low heat or till rice is fully cooked.

* Basmati rice is a thin long grain rice. These grains should be washed 3 times in a bowl with warm water. The first wash will leave milky water which is drained off. After the third washing the water should be clear. This indicates the rice is clear of any white starch and therefore will not stick together when cooked.

Ghee (Clarified Butter)

Ingredients:

1 lb salted or unsalted butter

Method:

1. Place butter in a saucepan on low heat.
2. Allow butter to melt and come to a rolling boil.
3. Do not stir. Continue boiling for 15 to 20 minutes or till froth reduces considerably and you can see a clear gold liquid.*
4. Remove pan from heat. Allow ghee to cool down.
5. Strain ghee through thick layers of cheesecloth into a glass jar.
6. Store ghee in a cool dry place.

*It is important for ghee to melt long enough to remove all milk solids. This will ensure that the ghee will not go rancid when stored in a cool dry place.

Condiments Masalas & Desserts

Condiments Masalas & Desserts

Spicy Tomato Sauce

Ingredients:

1 cup tomato ketchup
4 tablespoons cider vinegar
3 garlic cloves grated
½ teaspoon red chillie powder
2 teaspoons crushed cumin
1 teaspoon salt
1 tablespoon chopped cilantro

Method:

1.   Mix together in a bowl grated garlic, red chillie powder, crushed cumin, salt, chopped cilantro and cider vinegar.
2.   Add tomato ketchup and mix thoroughly.
3.   Store in the refrigerator and serve cold.

Cilantro Chutney

Ingredients:

3 bunches cilantro or 3 cups cilantro
2 green chillies (Serrano or Cayenne)
3 garlic cloves peeled
½ teaspoon coarse salt or sea salt
3 teaspoons cumin seeds
juice of one lemon
1 teaspoon salt

Method:

1.   Wash and drain cilantro in a colander.
2.   Place cilantro, green chillies, garlic cloves, cumin seeds and coarse salt or sea salt in a chopper or food processor. Blend till chutney is a smooth paste. Store chutney in the freezer in small sealed containers.
3.   Stir in lemon juice and 1 teaspoon salt just before serving.

Ginger/Garlic Masala

Ingredients:

1 cup freshly peeled garlic cloves
1 cup freshly peeled ginger
3 fresh green chillies (Serrano or Cayenne)
¼ teaspoon coarse salt

Method:

1.   Place garlic, ginger, green chillies and salt in a chopper or food processor. Blend till masala is a fine paste.
2.   Store ginger/garlic masala in the freezer. Fill small sealed containers or freezer bags with small amounts of masala. Seal and flatten bag, so that the masala is about ⅛ inch thick.
3.   When you require masala, break off the amount you need and place the masala back in the freezer.

Ginger/garlic masala is used in most of the dishes in this cookbook, as well as in the second and third cookbooks of this series.

Green Chillie Masala

Ingredients:

1 cup fresh green chillies (Serrano or Cayenne)
¼ teaspoon coarse salt

Method:

1.   Wash and drain green chillies.
2.   Place whole chillies and salt in a chopper or food processor. Process till masala looks like a paste.
3.   Store green chillie masala in the freezer. Fill sealed containers or freezer bags with small amounts of masala. Seal and flatten bag, so that masala is about ⅛ inch thick.
4.   When you require masala, break off the amount you need and place masala back in the freezer.

Green Chillie masala is used in most of the dishes in this cookbook, as well as in the second and third cookbooks of this series.

Garlic Masala

Ingredients:

1 cup fresh garlic cloves peeled
2 fresh green chillies (Serrano or Cayenne)
¼ teaspoon coarse salt

Method:

1.   Blend garlic, whole chillies and salt in a chopper or food processor, till masala is a fine paste.
2.   Store garlic masala in the freezer. Fill freezer bags with small amounts of masala. Seal and flatten the bag, so that masala is about ⅛ inch thick. When you require masala, just break off the amount you need and place masala back in the freezer.

Garlic masala is used in a few of the recipes in this cookbook, as well as in the second and third cookbooks of this series.

Cool Melon Dessert

Ingredients:

½ seedless watermelon
½ cantaloupe
½ honeydew melon
1 cup green seedless grapes
1 cup red seedless grapes
4 to 6 tablespoons honey
juice of half a lemon
4 tablespoons finely chopped mint

Method:

1. Remove seeds from cantaloupe and honeydew melons.
2. Using a melon baller, scoop out round balls of watermelon, cantaloupe and honeydew melons. Place in a large dessert bowl.
3. Add green and red grapes.
4. In a separate bowl mix together honey, lemon juice and mint.
5. Pour mixture over fruit. Toss.
6. Cover and place in fridge. Serve cold.

Raas Malai

Ingredients:

500g ricotta cheese
1 ¼ cups sugar
1 ½ litres half and half cream
1 ½ teaspoons ground cardamom
½ cup thinly sliced almonds
2 tablespoons crushed pistachios

Method:

1. Mix together ricotta cheese and ¼ cup of sugar.
2. Spread mixture thinly on a cookie sheet and bake at 300°F for 45 to 50 minutes.
3. Allow baked ricotta cheese to cool, then cut into small squares. Place squares in a large dessert dish.
4. In a large pot mix together half and half cream, 1 cup sugar and cardamom. Stir well.
5. Heat mixture on medium heat stirring occasionally. Bring mixture to a rolling boil.
6. Pour warm cream mixture over ricotta cheese. Stir in sliced almonds and crushed pistachios. Sprinkle ground cardamom to garnish.
7. Serve chilled.

Seero

Ingredients:

1 cup cream of wheat
4 tablespoons ghee
2 tablespoons brown sugar
¼ cup raisins (optional)
¼ cup chopped almonds
1 cup warm water
1 cup milk
1 teaspoon ground cardamom

Method:

1.   Heat ghee in a saucepan on medium heat. Add cream of wheat and stir continuously until golden brown.
2.   Add water and milk. Stir. Cover and allow to cook for 10 to 15 minutes, stirring occasionally.
3.   Add brown sugar, raisins, chopped almonds and cardamom. Stir well.
4.   Cook for a further 10 to 15 minutes on low heat, stirring frequently to avoid sticking.

Sev

Ingredients:

1 cup vermicelli pasta - broken
6 tablespoons ghee (page 82)
4 tablespoons brown sugar
¼ cup raisins (optional)
¼ cup chopped almonds
2 ½ cups water
1 teaspoon ground cardamom

Method:

1.	Heat ghee in a saucepan on medium heat. Add pasta and stir continuously until golden brown.
2.	Add water and stir. Cover and allow to cook for 10 to 15 minutes, stirring occasionally.
3.	Add brown sugar, raisins, chopped almonds and cardamom. Stir well.
4.	Cook for a further 15 to 20 minutes on low heat, stirring frequently to avoid sticking.

Notes

Measurement Charts, Meal Suggestions & Glossary

Measurement Charts, Meal Suggestions & Glossary

Measurement Conversion Chart

Temperature	
Celsius - °C	**Fahrenheit - °F**
150°C	300°F
175°C	350°F
190°C	375°F
205°C	400°F
220°C	425°F

Measurement Conversion Chart

Weight	
Metric	**Imperial**
250 g	½ 1b
454 g	1 lb
1 kg	2.2 lb
1.5 kg	3.3 lb
2.2 kg	4.8 lb

Measurement Conversion Chart

Volume	
Metric	**Imperial**
1.25 ml	¼ teaspoon
2.5 ml	½ teaspoon
5 ml	1 teaspoon
15 ml	1 tablespoon
62.5 ml	¼ cup
125 ml	½ cup
250 ml	1 cup

Meal Suggestions

MEAL - I	
Tandoori Chicken	37
Spicy Baked Potatoes	43
Herb Bread	44
Cilantro Chutney	86
Cool Melon Dessert	90
Traditional Chai (tea)	15

MEAL – II	
Barbecued Fish Steaks in Lettuce Leaf	39
Spicy Corn	59
Spicy Baked Potatoes	43
Cilantro Chutney	86
Cool Melon Dessert	90
Traditional Chai (tea)	15

MEAL – III	
Barbecued Chicken Kebabs	38
Barbecued Meat Balls	40
Herb Bread	44
Spicy Baked Potatoes	43
Cool Melon Dessert	90
Traditional Chai (tea)	15

Meal Suggestions

MEAL - IV	
Spicy Roasted Chicken	52
Spicy Corn	59
Basmati Rice	81
Spicy Tomato Sauce	85
Raas Malai	91
Traditional Chai (tea)	15

MEAL – V	
Spicy Meat Balls	17
Chicken Curry	49
Spicy Potatoes	61
Foolecha	78
Cilantro Chutney	86
Cool Melon Dessert	90
Traditional Chai (tea)	15

MEAL - VI	
Spicy Fish	54
Shrimp Curry	53
Spicy Corn	59
Naan	79
Spicy Tomato Sauce	85
Traditional Chai (tea)	15

Meal Suggestions

MEAL – VII	
Moothya (Spicy Patties)	18
Eggplant Potato Curry	57
Plain Roti (Chapatti)	80
Seero	92
Traditional Chai (tea)	15

MEAL - VIII	
Spicy Pepper and Potato Dish	60
Mung Bean Curry	68
Basmati Rice	81
Flaky Roti (Chapatti)	75
Raas Malai	91
Traditional Chai (tea)	15

MEAL – IX	
Spicy Spinach Rolls (Patarya)	16
Spicy Black Eyed Beans	70
Basmati Rice	81
Spicy Tomato Sauce	85
Raas Malai	91
Traditional Chai (tea)	15

Meal Suggestions

MEAL – X	
Pan Roasted Potatoes	29
Chicken Curry	49
Spicy Corn	59
Foolecha	78
Basmati Rice	81
Cilantro Chutney	86
Traditional Chai (tea)	15

MEAL – XI	
Vadas	20
Chicken Pilaf	47
Zucchini with Chana Daal	69
Spicy Corn	59
Raas Malai	91
Traditional Chai (tea)	15

Glossary

All spices, spice blends and cookware needed for Indian cooking mentioned in this glossary are available from Daksha's Gourmet Spices at www.spicesgourmet.com

Ajwain seeds	carom seeds
Baste	to moisten food with fat or other liquids whilst cooking
Bake	to cook by dry heat inside an oven
Basmati rice	thin long grained rice
Bhajyas	appetizers made with chana flour and chopped vegetables also known as Pakoras
Bind	to thicken liquids by the addition of thickening agents
Black Mustard Seed	used in many appetizers and vegetable dishes
Blend	mix ingredients together
Boil	cook food in large amounts of liquid till it bubbles
Cardamom	green pods with aromatic black seeds
Cassia sticks	the outer bark of a cinnamon tree
Chai	tea
Chai masala	spice mixture to make spicy tea
Chana	chick peas
Chapatti	thin flat Indian bread also known as Roti
Chop	cut up in small pieces
Chutney	spicy condiment made with vegetables or fruit
Chevtee Daal	daal made with a mixture of different lentils
Cilantro	herb grown from coriander seeds
Clarify	to remove impurities from a liquid or fat by heating, skimmering and straining
Cumin	also known as jeeroo, commonly used in Indian dishes
Daal	husked split beans
Deep Fry	cook food by immersing in sufficient hot oil to cover food
Dice	cut into small cubes

Glossary

Dokra	spicy steamed lentil cake
Drizzle	pour liquid very slowly to gently cover food
Fenugreek	bitter brown seeds also known as methi
Fillet	cut off piece of raw meat or fish removing skin and bones
Foolecha	small round fried bread made with spices, yeast and flour
Fry	to cook in small amount of fat in an open pan
Garam	warm
Garam masala	warm mixture - a blend of many spices
Garnish	decorate and flavor a dish with spices or herbs
Ghee	clarified butter
Grate	reduce food to small strips by rubbing on serrated surface
Jullienned	to cut vegetables in thin long strips
Jeeroo	cumin seeds
Knead	work dough by folding and stretching with heel of hand
Marinate	soak food in seasoned liquid or paste to tenderize and flavor before cooking
Masala	mixture
Moothya	round patties shaped by hand and pan fried
Naan	leavened flat bread also known as pita bread
Pakoras	bhajyas
Patarya	spicy spinach rolls
Pilaf	cooked rice with vegetables and or meat
Puri	crispy deep fried bread
Red Chillie Powder	made from crushed hot cayenne red peppers
Roast	cook with little fat in an oven
Roti	flat bread also known as Chapatti
Samosa	triangular shaped pastry filled with a thick spicy curry
Sauté	cook food gently in a little fat in an open pan

Glossary

Seero	sweet dessert made with semolina
Serrano	type of green chillie pepper
Sev	sweet dessert made with very thin pasta
Sieve	pass liquid or dried food through a fine mesh to remove lumps
Steam	cook in steam from boiling liquid
Strain	to filter
Tawa	traditional Indian concave shaped pan without an edge, made for cooking roti or naan bread
Thana	coriander seeds
Toower	pigeon peas
Tumeric powder	bright yellow root, dried and ground
Urad	black mung beans
Vadas	fried crispy appetizers in the shape of little round balls
Vadhu	curry made with sprouted beans
Velan	thin oval shaped rolling pin for rolling rotis and naan bread

Notes

Notes

Notes

Notes

Notes

Notes

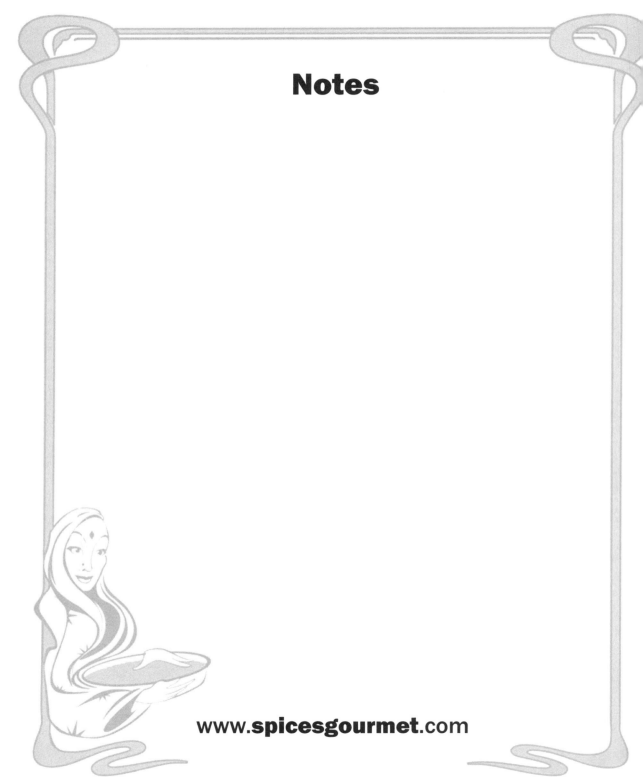